Getting Clean is EASY!

Staying Clean is the Challenge!

Author: A.L. Cartwright

ISBN: 9798851041419

Copyright Registration: TXu 2-381-041

Table of Contents

Intro

This manual is dedicated to all my fellow addicts on the quest to seek a change that will stand the test of time. This is not written from an academic point of view. My knowledge about what works in recovery comes because I have lived it. During active addiction, I have been down to depths that some of you could not even imagine. The lowest of lows. For years I was a slave to my addiction. I was caught up in a vicious cycle of relapse and recovery. From there I have put together over three decades clean. I have seen the struggle from both sides. I have come back from depths that few have come back from and live to tell about, to having over thirty years on the other side clean and sober. Because of this, I am compelled to share my experience, strength, and hope to all addicts who are struggling and need to know that it can be done.

Addict?

Are you an addict? This is a question one must have a definitive answer to before any real, extended clean time can be established. To answer this question takes some honest introspection and soul searching. My definition of an addict is a person whose life has become unmanageable as a result of any mood or mind-altering substances, habits or behaviors. Many struggle with **staying** clean simply because they have not honestly answered this question within themselves. They analyze, rationalize, and minimize their situation until they reach a bottom of some kind. That is when they finally face the fact that they are, indeed, an addict. Until an addict faces this reality, progress in recovery is usually limited and short lived. Until one reaches this conclusion, any recovery efforts are usually not met with the necessary conviction, commitment, dedication, and most importantly motivation. All of which are necessary to put together any substantial amount of clean time. Are you an addict? The answer to this question will set the course of your journey in recovery.

"KNOWING YOURSELF IS THE BEGINNING OF ALL WISDOM"

— ARISTOTLE

Getting Clean is Easy

Getting clean is easy. As addicts, when we recognize we have a problem, we begin to take steps to address it, we get "clean". We get caught up in the vicious cycle of relapse/recovery, getting clean over and over again. Getting clean is a great first step, but getting clean is not the solution. Getting clean is the easy part. **Staying** clean is the challenge! I managed to get "clean" many times. I've only managed to stay clean once, which is where I am today, over 34 years clean, one day at a time.

To put together any substantial amount of clean time, you must change your self-talk. Stop saying you want to get clean and start saying, "I want to **Stay** clean." Just that small shift in perspective will be of immense help on your recovery journey. It's definitely a balancing act to think long term, while staying grounded in today. Today is truly all we have, because the journey truly is one day at a time.

" NOTHING CHANGES IF NOTHING CHANGES"

Toolbox Approach

When it comes to **staying** clean, there are different approaches, different theories, different philosophies, and different techniques. So many different schools of thought. In my experience, I have found that they are all right!

In my decades of experience being clean, on my journey in recovery, I have found that there is not one particular thing that keeps you clean. You have to pull something from them all. Life is complex and unpredictable, so you never know what approach will serve you best in any given situation. I liken it to a worker coming to a construction site with his tools. The more tools he has in his toolbox, the more effective he will be at his task. Embrace every approach, every philosophy, every technique. They all have something of value to offer. Relying too heavily on one approach leaves you vulnerable. Humans are complex beings, life is complex. Your recovery should be approached the same way. Recovery is not a "one size fits all" endeavor. That cookie cutter approach to recovery diminishes your odds of long-term success. Be open minded and receptive to all the tools of recovery.

Remember, if you only bring a hammer to a job site, you can only pound nails! Fill up your recovery toolbox with as many tools as possible. Here are some examples of the tools of recovery that can be used:

-12 step program.	-stress management.
-anger management.	-counseling.
-gratitude practice.	-affirmations.
-visualization.	-journaling.
-spiritual/religious.	-group therapy
-behavior modification.	-exercise.
-meditation.	-awareness practice.
-helping others.	-individual therapy.

These are just a few basic examples of some tools to put in your recovery toolbox. Each person is unique, so each person can add many more tools to their box. Remember, the more tools you have and use, the better your chances of **staying** clean long term. The key to adding or expanding the number of tools in your recovery toolbox is to be open minded. Don't close the door on any approach, method or technique. Don't give more weight to one approach over another. Don't underestimate or minimize any one particular tool. Because the tool that gets you through one part of your journey may not be the tool that gets you through the next. The recovery method, technique or approach you think of as insignificant, may be the very thing that gets you through a crisis.

So be open minded, embrace them all. Every tool you have will have its day at the top of the list if you stay clean long enough. Longevity in recovery depends on your use of different methods, different techniques, different approaches.

" CHANGE BEGINS WHERE YOUR COMFORT ZONE ENDS"

It Takes a Village

The old saying, "It take a village", really applies when it comes to recovery from addiction. A recovering addict's "village" is their support system. A support system is vital to recovery. It is a lifeline for recovering addicts.

For those addicts who are fortunate enough to have a support system in place at the start of their recovery journey, lean into it, embrace it, nurture it. For those of you who don't, no worries! Because building a support system in recovery is easy. Support groups are everywhere, and you will be surprised how others will reach out to help you when you are trying to do the right thing. It doesn't matter if you have a support system in place or have to build your own, a support system is indispensable on your journey in recovery.

Support in recovery comes in many forms. It can come in the form of support groups, 12 step programs, group therapy, recovery social circles, and so on. When you put together some clean time, you will be a magnet for those willing to help you. When others feel you are making a sincere effort to stay clean, they will rally around you. The right people will show up in your life, and situations of benefit will unexpectedly appear. I have seen it happen time and time again, to others as well as myself. You just have to take that first step and reach out. Just remember, when building a support system, make a conscious effort to include someone who will give you honest feedback, someone who will tell you what you need to hear, not just what you want to hear. With a support system in place, your odds of putting together a substantial amount clean time skyrocket.

" SURROUND YOURSELF WITH POSITIVE PEOPLE"

Triggers

In order to put together any substantial amount of clean time, you must understand your triggers. Triggers are anything that can instantly or gradually trigger a response that leads to a relapse. Triggers can be anything from people to places or things. Triggers can be subtle or obvious. To understand your triggers takes some self-honesty and some soul searching. Every addict has triggers. Avoiding them at all costs greatly increases your chances of putting together a substantial amount of clean time. Know your triggers, make a list of them, face them honestly.

There's an old saying in recovery that states you have to change people, places, and things in order to have success. This helps tremendously on your journey because it is a broad way of avoiding all triggers. For those that are not able to change all three at once, making an effort to narrow down or pinpoint your specific triggers is necessary on your journey.

It's amazing how things come together for you in the early stages of recovery when you stay out of your own way by avoiding your triggers.

" UNDERSTANDING YOURSELF IS POWERFUL"

Magic of Exercise*

In my experience, one of the most underrated parts of any recovery program is exercise. Exercise helps in so many ways. Exercise helps you mentally, physically, psychologically, and spiritually. I don't think there is anything else that helps recovery from addiction in so many different ways. Exercise doesn't mean running a marathon or lifting heavy weights. It can be something as simple as walking or just moving with intention. Most everyone can do something. Without getting too scientific, it is a fact that our bodies function better when we are active. We were created to move. Exercise also helps relieve the stress and anxiety that naturally occurs during the recovery process. It helps improve bodily functions in many ways. It helps you mentally by giving you something to feel good about, that self-esteem boost that recovering addicts need during the recovery process. It helps you beyond the physical by increasing that mind/body connection that is spiritually so important to addicts.

Exercise also releases that feel good chemical in your brain. That same chemical that addicts are chasing during active addiction. I have found that during the early stages of recovery, the urges and cravings to relapse were less frequent and less intense when I exercised. I really feel that without consistent and intentional exercise, I couldn't have put together the amount of time clean I have up to this point.

Exercise is also a way of expressing self-love, something to feel good about. Each time you exercise with intention is a small victory in your quest to stay clean. **Staying** clean is nothing more than putting together a series of small victories one day at a time. Putting together a series of small victories is how you turn the tide on your addiction. *Disclaimer: make sure you are medically cleared before starting any exercise program.

"TAKE CARE OF YOUR BODY ITS THE ONLY PLACE YOU HAVE TO LIVE"

Don't Resist a Good Habit

On our journey in recovery, we must be conscious of our habits. Habits are formed whether we are conscious of them or not. We must give attention and intention to the habits we form. We know intuitively if a habit is good for us or not. Forming new and beneficial habits takes effort. They take us out of our comfort zone. Therefore, we naturally resist good habits.

We must become conscious and aware of the habits we form, especially in the early stages of recovery. If you don't pay attention to forming good habits, the old habits and patterns that kept you in negative cycles will creep in. Those old habits and patterns were comfortable and familiar. They can creep back in easily with no effort at all. Being conscious and aware of your habits allows you to form good habits. Stay positive and intentionally form good habits, and the old negative habits will ease their way out. It is far more powerful to run towards something than to run away from something. Always try to focus on what you are trying to achieve, not what you are trying to avoid.

" FIRST, WE FORM HABITS, THEN THEY FORM US"

More Powerful to Run Towards Something than Away from Something

Although it is important not to forget your lows during active addiction, you must not dwell on them. Instead, focus on what you want your life to look like during recovery. One day at a time is still the best approach. The practice of visualization plays a key role in recovery when it comes to looking forward, and not focusing on the past. The practice of visualization involves holding a mental picture of the things you want to manifest in your life. Start each day visualizing what you want that day clean to look like. Focus on what you are moving toward. The practice of visualization should be one of the tools of recovery in every addict's recovery toolbox. It is definitely a balancing act to be able to look forward, while staying grounded in today.

In the early stages of recovery, it is also important to stay in a state of gratitude. Even if it is something small. Start your day with an "I am grateful" mindset. Gratitude is a powerful tool to have in recovery toolbox. It is amazing how quickly things will come together for you when you stay in gratitude. One day at a time, look forward not behind you. Focus on what you are moving toward, not what you are running from.

"THE SECRET OF CHANGE IS TO FOCUS ALL OF YOUR ENERGY NOT ON FIGHTING THE OLD, BUT ON BUILDING THE NEW"

SOCRATES

Replace Your Addictions

As addicts, we have addictive personalities, but all addictions are not destructive. You can replace your destructive behavior with positivity. There are many positive things you can gravitate towards. You can be addictive about helping others, addictive about self-improvement, addictive about your recovery program. Make a list of things you think are positive behaviors. Embrace them, make them habits. Lock-in to those positive addictions and give them time, one day at a time. Be all about "**Staying Clean**", not just getting clean.

Embrace your addictive personality, it's who you are, but use this knowledge as a force for good. Move towards constructive behaviors. Cultivate constructive behaviors with intent. Longevity on the quest to stay clean depends on it.

" THE TRUTH IS YOU DONT BREAK A BAD HABIT, YOU REPLACE IT WITH A GOOD ONE"

DENIS WAITLEY

Total Abstinence

For those of us who are truly addicts with addictive personalities, total abstinence dramatically increases your odds of putting together a substantial amount of clean time. Thinking that you could taper down to manageable levels or socially indulge is a "Fool yourself" approach that will lead you back to square one. Indulgence is like lighting a fuse, sooner or later there will be an explosion. Remember, getting clean is easy, **staying** clean is the challenge. In all my years in recovery, I have yet to see any addict "control their active addiction". Abstinence is best approached with a one day at a time or a just for today mindset. The days will add up before you know it. Trying to think about total abstinence too far out in the future can be stressful and overwhelming. Just conquer each day as it comes. Approach total abstinence with a sense of pride and sense of strength. Being able to abstain from anything intentionally is a sense of strength.

The best way to remain abstinent is to not put yourself in situations that may be compromising, especially early on in recovery. Life is complex enough, so don't get in your own way. Keep it simple by just controlling what you can control. Longevity in abstinence is nothing more than a series of small victories day by day, hour by hour, sometimes minute by minute.

Take pride in total abstinence, wear it like a badge of honor. Be quick to say no in slippery situations. You will be surprised how much respect and compliments you will receive from those around you. You don't have to disclose your reasons for abstaining to anyone outside of your support circle. Remember, it's always best to stay out of slippery situations altogether. Abstinence plays a key role in "staying" clean long term.

" TODAYS MIGHTY OAK IS YESTERDAY'S NUT THAT HELD ITS GROUND"

Do it for You

Many addicts start their "clean" journey for reasons outside of themselves. Most of the time it is our circumstances becoming unmanageable that forces us to seek change. It may be family or friends that motivate or encourage us to seek change, and that's great for motivating us to start the journey to get clean, and initially it works. But, getting clean is the easy part, **staying** clean is another story. No matter who or what motivated you to get clean; in order to stay clean, you have to do it for you! To put together any substantial stretch of extended clean time, you **must** want it for yourself. Because eventually, any outside motivation wears off. Unless you are motivated from within, longevity on your journey to remain clean will prove to be elusive. If you are going to go far on your journey in recovery, No one can want it for you, more than you want it for yourself!

Even if you started your clean journey for reasons outside of yourself, you could internalize that motivation and make it your own. This can be accomplished by taking conscious and deliberate actions to elevate your self-worth. The more you begin to value yourself, the less you will want to engage in behaviors that are self-destructive. As a result, you will become motivated from within to want to stay clean. No matter how you get there, you must be motivated from within to achieve longevity on your quest to stay clean. You have to do it for "You!"

" TURN YOUR WOUNDS INTO WISDOM"

OPRAH

Conclusion

Recovery is a journey, not a destination. The principles in this manual are proven to work long term when applied as a whole. Being clean and sober long term is possible. It can be achieved. With over 34 years clean at the time of this writing, I am proof!

45572583R00022